DO THE
WORK

ALSO BY GARY JOHN BISHOP

Unf*ck Yourself

Stop Doing That Sh*t

DO THE
WORK

The Official Unrepentant, Ass-Kicking, No-Kidding, Change-Your-Life Sidekick to *Unf*ck Yourself*

GARY JOHN BISHOP

First published in Great Britain in 2019 by Yellow Kite
An imprint of Hodder & Stoughton
An Hachette UK company

First published in the United States of America in
2019 by HarperOne, an imprint of HarperCollins

2

Designed by Billie Gaura / 212 Degrees

A CIP catalogue record for this title is
available from the British Library

Trade Paperback ISBN 978 1 529 31775 6
eBook ISBN 978 1 529 31981 1

Printed and bound in Great Britain by Clays Ltd, Elcograf S.p.A.

Hodder & Stoughton policy is to use papers that are
natural, renewable and recyclable products and made
from wood grown in sustainable forests. The logging and
manufacturing processes are expected to conform to the
environmental regulations of the country of origin.

Yellow Kite
Hodder & Stoughton Ltd
Carmelite House
50 Victoria Embankment
London EC4Y 0DZ

www.yellowkitebooks.co.uk

Contents

01

INTRODUCTION

You are not defined by what's inside your head. You are what you do. **Your actions.**

—Unf*ck Yourself, p. 117

I'm not a fan of self-help workbooks or journals or planners.

I mean, they're okay, and sure, they might work for some people, but here's the deal, they never worked for me. If you've used them before and you're reading this, there's a good chance they never really worked for you either.

In my case, I would get bored or distracted or caught up in the drama of my real life and eventually give up. Another failure to add to the list. They just seemed too powder puff, too generic to get to the heart of my shit and so I'd quit.

Ah well, there's always hope I guess . . . and Amazon Prime.

What I am a big fan of is helping people take their lives on once and for all. To empower them to call quits on their own bullshit. And that's why I wrote this.

You see, the problem with taking your life on is that you somehow think you know what you need to do. At least at some level. And that's usually what you've got in mind whenever you take on changing something about your life. You think if you just had more money, less worry, more patience, more confidence, then life would be amazing, or at the very least, better. You say to yourself, I need love, I need to move, I need a break, blah de blah, blah, blah. But in my experience of people, they have often conflated and distorted their lives to such a degree that they lack the kind of mental clarity and decisiveness they need to be able to point to something and categorically state,

THAT THING RIGHT THERE, THAT'S A GAME CHANGER!

I mean, think about it. If you really had worked your shit out you'd be living the life you are after already and you're not, you're sitting reading these words. That, at least, should tell you something.

So here we now are.

An *Unf*ck Yourself* workbook with an emphasis on the *work* part.

Be left in no doubt, that's what this is. A personal workshop for your brain, a legit resource where you can work your life out, what matters to you, what's going to make the biggest difference and empower you to act in ways that make some palpable change to the direction your life is currently taking. This book is all about mastering the head game of the change you say you want to make. Get this down and suddenly the pathway gets a lot clearer.

Where do we start? Well, try on the idea that you go through life with a myriad of unfinished business on your mind. Unanswered emails, the frayed edges of old friendships, soured emotions and relationships, regrets about career, anger and anxiety and numbness about the mountain of things you are getting over, getting past, promising you'll get back to or finally take on and all of it mangled into the stress and survival of the life you're currently trying to wade through to some sort of success or happiness.

Your capacity for taking life on, the kind of mental space required for you to be your greatest, most effective self, is compressed and squeezed into whatever scraps of room you have available in your head AFTER all that other shit has had its way with you before it retreats to the vast and luscious piece of prime real estate it occupies in the recesses of your mind. And it will be back. Oh yeah, that shit isn't done with you yet.

It's like a pot of water that boils then cools then boils then cools then boils repeatedly and the only peace of mind you get is when the heat is off. When it's on? Oh dear.

That last argument with your sister? It'll be back. Your fear of writing that book? Hello! I'm over here! Your credit report? *cough* Car loan application. Your shitty childhood, your lack of purpose, your ex, your body shape, your dad/mom/boss/dead dog . . . whatever you might think you're momentarily okay with or getting over or trying to forget will come up out of nowhere and give you the old back-of-the-hand every now and again just to keep you in line.

Wine—yeah, that's the answer. Eh . . . no.

WHAT WE'RE DOING HERE

I don't do things the way everyone else does them, and with this book, I wanted to give you something different, something that was a little more in line with my "urban philosophy" approach and that gives you a pathway to take a deep plunge into the dark of your own little mystery of life. If you've read *Unf*ck Yourself* once or a million times or even just read some quotes on Instagram, this will sound familiar to you.

But it's easy to read something and then go on to the next thing in our day and forget about that great thing you read that maybe just could change your life. So in this book I've broken life down into some simple key elements.

In *Unf*ck Yourself*, I showed you how it's often the conversation that we're in with ourselves, the negative self-talk, that keeps us making the same bad choices over and over and over. And I gave you seven simple-to-use pathways to interrupt the negative self-talk.

The seven assertions, remember?

Here, you'll get the opportunity to dive in and get to the bottom of some of your most important "stuff," to put a doorstop in that negative conversation, to finally forge a clear pathway to the life you're after. Wouldn't it be great if you could reveal the things that are going to make the most difference, the kind of things you could easily point to, and declare, "Yep, I unfucked myself there"?

We're going to dive headlong into the shit pile and focus specifically on what doesn't work in your life, why it doesn't work (really), and what it's going to take from you to turn this around.

And that's what makes this workbook so different. It's not a planner (use your phone or the calendar hanging up in your parents' kitchen for that stuff, and yes, it's that easy to plan shit). This isn't some kind of inspiration handbook. If you need a quick jolt of wake-the-fuck up, pick a random chapter of *Unf*ck Yourself* and plow in; you'll have more inspiration than you can handle.

I'm also not out to have you take on yet another complex strategy for winning at an already complex life. This isn't the three/five/seven secrets to success or some corny acronym you'll need to remember every time you get out of bed, and no, WTF doesn't mean Wise, Talented, and Fantastic.

For what it's worth I'll never write a book about the three steps to happiness, for instance. Mainly because I'm pretty convinced two of those steps are pizza and a martini.

Here you will simply answer questions. Lots of them. I've taken so many people through questions just like these and seen how when the person really takes the time to answer them honestly and completely, life change can happen. Often spectacularly so. These questions are designed to provoke and reveal whatever you have suppressed or tried to minimize, the kind of things one might throw into the backpack of a life and carry around until the weight becomes too much. It is critical that you give these questions real thinking. You might need to dwell on some of them for a few minutes, others for a day or two. One-word answers will NOT suffice. Your answers will require you to get specific and to get in touch with your most pressing of human concerns, the stuff that lurks in the underworld of your emotions, below the surface of your excuses and justifications and explanations.

I'm out to provide you with something that will simplify your life and empower the incredible shit you are up to or at least, could be up to. The answer will be in your answers. Literally. So make sure you give them your full attention and commitment.

BREAKING IT DOWN

There are three segments we'll go through together in this workbook:

SELF

PEOPLE

PURPOSE

They cover the primary areas of life that a person will suffer through, struggle with, or get stuck with. These are the things that they tolerate about themselves, how they mindlessly navigate relationships, and the ways they fudge their way through what their life is really all about.

I want you to know, I get you. I know what it is to *be* you because I *am* you. I might not be the same age as you or the same gender or have the same past, but we share the critical component that unites us all. We are all human *beings*, and when you start to relate to each other's ways of *being*, the mystery of human relatedness opens up like a lotus flower. In other words, I got your back.

HONESTLY, REALLY?

There are two absolutely crucial ingredients you'll need to participate in this workbook in any sort of meaningful way.

One thing you will need is a genuine and unmistakable *honesty* with yourself.

Most people believe that they *are* honest with themselves when in fact they are just not.

Try on the idea that you are a liar.

I really mean that.

You lie to yourself. You are a liar and a withholder and a pretender. Now, before you charge headlong to your local offend-a-center to rent your own little self-righteous bus and scurry off to Twitterville for support, let me expand a little.

How many times have you told yourself you're okay with something when you're just not? *"It's nothing, it doesn't matter."* Suuuuuure it doesn't. Keep pedaling, Braveheart.

How about those times when you say you can't when deep down you know you totally can? *"I'll definitely do it, just not now, that's all. I've got a lot going on."* Yeah . . . a lot going on, that's the ticket.

Then there are those occasions when you say you will but you already know you won't. *"I'll try."* Oh well, God loves a trier, huh?

Now I'm not saying all of this to piss you off and make you start arguing with this page in the middle of the shampoo aisle at Walmart. I'm saying this so you can confront your own bullshit. You, my friend, are full of it and you are full of it with yourself. You have become enslaved by your own feelings and excuses and become so entrenched in your own web of deceit and head fakes that you actually believe most of the shit you tell yourself. To you, this unreal shit is real!

At times you'll even fight for it too. The mock-rage levels can reach peak performance to hide the truth, right? I haven't even started to talk about those things that you're ashamed of or guilty about or still trying to forget, but they are included here too. This downright fakery has to end in these pages. This workbook will be a complete waste of your time if you cannot bring yourself to the truth. This is your opportunity to tell one on yourself with no consequences. To experience the relief and clarity that arise when you are finally straight with yourself about yourself. The best part is you can do it all in the solitude and privacy of these pages.

To sum it all up, every single last question in this workbook has to be answered with complete, 100 percent honesty, with nothing left out.

A PROMISE KEPT

Next up, your *promises*. Your promises aren't worth shit. If that offends you, so what? You can't keep getting offended at everything that touches a nerve. Perhaps it's time to start understanding your emotional charges rather than indulging them at every turn.

Look, the reason your promises are so weak is down to a lifetime of bending, breaking, changing, and abandoning them. Even you know when you make a promise that it's not really a promise. It's more like a well-intentioned statement that might or might not happen depending on the weather, money, time, feelings, moods, things going well, etc., etc., etc.

Over time, your relationship to what you say has become diluted, lacking in any real substance or personal power. And then you wonder why your life doesn't work! You may even find yourself actively avoiding making any kind of promises to make sure you always leave a backdoor for yourself. Y'know, no commitment, no looking bad, right?

Even if you *do* make promises, they're the kind of cozy ones that you know you can fairly reliably keep. Talk about living in your comfort zone! Just so we're clear, I continually make bold promises that go beyond what I think I can do and then turn my life inside out to keep them. I'm constantly raising the bar with myself. It's usually an uncomfortable, annoying, frustrating, and uncertain ride but ultimately fulfilling and empowering. I love that I get to do that with my life.

Ever hear the phrase, "Never make a promise you can't keep"? Fuck that! Bring it on! You have to *love* making those kinds of bold commitments.

Your sense of personal power is directly correlated to the strength of the relationship between you and what you say. Keeping your personal promises is the single most underused, undervalued, and ignored source of power for people.

Turning your life around will require you to start holding your promises above *all* else. Why? Because your promises don't have feelings to consider; they also don't care about the weather or how much money there is or what people think. They stand there alone in the universe, calling you to be your greatest self. To entice and sometimes demand that you act in your life, especially when you are most denying or resisting or hiding from them. Your promises are the future, your feelings, the past, and that's the choice you will have to make every day between now and when you die.

To really get what I mean when I say how crucial it is to start making bold promises, here's the definition of a *promise*:

- *a declaration that one will do or refrain from doing something specified.*
- *a legally binding declaration that gives the person to whom it is made a right to expect or to claim the performance or forbearance of a specified act.*

You'll notice it doesn't mention the word "unless" anywhere. It also doesn't say anything about excuses or reasons (genuine or otherwise) or how you feel or even the slightest mention of the odds being for or against you. Nope, not a word about your temper or sadness or lack of this or lack of that, not even a hint about your special situation or a smidgeon about the "impossible" people in your life who you would swear are holding you back either.

If you look back in your life, you'll see that every single personal failure of yours was a function of some broken promise. Something you set out to do but somewhere along the line you and that commitment, that promise, got stopped by some seemingly insurmountable thing, some circumstance or event that allowed you to say "enough" and then you ended it. You might have seduced yourself with a compelling change of direction or sought agreement from others for the absolute validity of your quitting. Your problem has been that you have fooled yourself into believing it was something other than you. Then you become a victim to it, just like everyone else is.

It's all *you* and your *promises*. Everything else is noise. If you got just *that* from this workbook, you'd be completely unstoppable.

Transforming your life will absolutely-no-kidding require you to transform how you relate to what you promise. Expose yourself to bold and enlivening promises and your life will soar like a bird. Hide from them and it's business as usual. It's that simple and it's that black and white. And that's exactly what we're going to do throughout these pages. In each section, you will make a promise, with concrete terms and real consequences, and then see how that changes how you approach these areas of your life.

I know that's not how the vast majority of society sees it. I know that many people want to talk about complexities and different circumstances and obstacles and the uniqueness of what they are dealing with, but if a blind man can make himself the profound promise of climbing Mount Everest and then force himself to deal with everything that would prevent him from doing so, you can handle whatever might be in your way from time to time.

The guy's name is Erik Weihenmayer, by the way; look him up. He climbed that fucking mountain.

LAST BUT NOT LEAST

Take this workbook on in the order it is presented. Do not skip anything even if you feel as if you already are doing okay in that area. You might be surprised at how *not* okay certain areas of your life actually are. You can also repeat the sections as many times as you see necessary over days, weeks, months, or even years. This simple methodology is both timeless and extremely effective. Have your copy of *Unf*ck Yourself* handy; it will help with some of the more challenging aspects of what we will reveal here. Oh, and bring a highlighter, pen, pencil, eraser, Post-it notes, and some spare paper too.

You may well need them to help you with some no-holds-barred honesty and to keep your damn promises.

02

PROJECT 1: A QUESTION OF SELF

*How willing are you to consider that your life is the way it is, not because of the weight of your circumstances or situation but rather **the weight of self-talk that pulls you down?***

—Unf*ck Yourself, p. 14

If you've ever felt like you lack confidence, or that you're too angry, or perhaps you're someone who is nice to a fault, or that you're too cold or disconnected, or too independent or different, misunderstood, or harsh or even unloved, you're not alone.

We all have aspects of ourselves that we seemingly can't get past or get over. Our weaknesses and faults, apparent shortages of personality or character, stifled emotions or certain behaviors that seem to come easily to others but are problematic to us.

We all have these little (and not-so-little) dark spots in our makeup, internalized faults that we know are there, and then we proceed to mold our entire life around them to avoid chaos or sadness or tragedy. Out of hopelessness or whatever, we let them dominate and push us into avoiding or resisting certain things we would otherwise take on and embrace.

For instance, people who seemingly lack confidence or feel like they're different or don't quite fit in simply might not pick up the phone when someone calls because they don't feel secure enough or open enough to deal with other people sometimes. The unease and the social awkwardness kick in and take over. Sometimes they're not even clear why they won't answer those calls; they're just not "feeling it."

They'll maybe play phone tag or stick to text messages, or on some days, simply disappear. "I'm not confident enough to do this" or "I'm introverted. What do they expect?"

That shit can grow arms and legs too. You can become isolated. Alone.

Of course, this is an innocent example of that particular personal constraint, but the old vote of "no confidence" can completely wreck a fledgling love or lay waste to the most brilliant and creative of ideas. It can become the mud from which a person never quite manages to shake free their longing-to-dance feet.

Alternatively, maybe you're someone who feels like you're *too* nice or *too* kind and therefore you're avoiding certain people for another reason entirely! Perhaps you feel as if you're constantly being taken advantage of and you can't bring yourself to take a stand for what matters to you, to say "no" or to push back on those you feel push you. So you smile or say something semiagreeable and slither awkwardly through the conversation to something else that's a little more comfortable or safe while that minivolcano erupts in your gut.

You might already have started handling this by limiting your participation in life and putting a lid on yourself. The familiar emotional garrote. A by-product of this approach is that you unknowingly turn yourself into a victim all too easily. You quietly blame others when you get yourself too close to that discomfort zone of yours. The quiet resentment can often go unnoticed.

Like it's something *they* need to change about themselves rather than a problem you need to handle on your own.

You think people are too pushy? Maybe that's something you need to start dealing with rather than retreating from. And no, I don't mean start speaking your mind either. That's the other end of an already destructive spectrum. Those of us who feel we're too stupid, simply not smart or talented enough, are going to avoid things we perceive as too challenging in specific areas. We're going to sidestep learning new or seemingly complex things. We'll stick to watching TV or gouging through social media instead of reading or acquiring new and important skills or strategies. We'll change the subject instead of trying to understand a difficult topic or one we have no knowledge of. We'll get lost in the ordinary of an otherwise extraordinary opportunity. The opportunity of being fully alive.

And how many of us avoid putting ourselves "out there" with people we're fond of or attracted to? How many of us are afraid or nervous of taking the initiative in a relationship, whether it's an existing one or just a connection we're hoping to build? That's sometimes the action of someone who might, at a primal level, feel unloved, unattractive, or unwanted. Then there's the longing. Oh boy, the longing for something powerful and intimate tempered by the yawning gap between our own insecurities and the fantastic land of a fully blossomed love.

Again, we all have these aspects of ourselves, though they're different for everyone. And to some extent, we all know we have them. We're conscious of them, no matter how fleetingly.

In fact, in our modern age, some people even have a weird sort of pride about these parts of themselves. They seem to embolden and reinforce their most negative aspects by indulging the drama of their temper or their laziness, as if somehow losing control of their emotions or avoiding work is conspiring to work in their favor. The pretense of "I don't care" is both juvenile and so obviously fake.

But it's the way these issues truly control our lives that we never see. This is the unconscious aspect. We never see how big and wide an impact this is having on everything we do and don't do. We never notice how pervasive it is in our lives, how it has infected every little nook and cranny of our day-to-day.

We hide all these issues behind excuses. We have so many excuses, one for everything that we want to avoid doing so that we don't have to face the actual problem. It's hard to see that the actual problem is, in fact, an excuse.

This phenomenon is best described as "tolerating ourselves." We tolerate our procrastination, our anger, our lack of confidence. We tolerate our anxiety or our niceness. We tolerate and then organize our lives around it like some sort of sacred effigy, the he/she who must be obeyed and never questioned.

We know that we have these problems, but instead of making the effort necessary to change them, we simply go along with them. And then they affect every aspect of our lives, from our job to our relationships to our passions.

They're like the tentacles of a big, nasty octopus. But this octopus has endless limbs with a monstrous reach that's stretching all throughout our lives, sticking and pushing and prodding and grabbing. There's a tentacle hitting snooze on our alarm, silencing our phone, covering our eyes, and rummaging through our desk.

But we don't see the connections. We view all of these issues as simply part of who we are, not realizing they all stem from the same source. But wouldn't it be great if we could finally name the source, and by doing so, empower ourselves to actually do something to cut off these poisonous tentacles?

Now, there's something to be said for "accepting yourself," both your strengths and your weaknesses. Especially when those apparent weaknesses are something you can't apparently change, such as your height or a physical disability.

But that doesn't mean the chronic procrastinator should resign themselves to procrastination; that he should continue to tolerate putting off work, dentist's appointments, and plans with friends because "I'm just a procrastinator."

The opposite of tolerating your issues isn't hating yourself or being insecure about who you are. In fact, many of these things are actually rooted in a fundamental insecurity. That you lack confidence, or feel unloved, or procrastinate is thanks to some hidden, subconscious, limiting beliefs about yourself.

If you want to change, you need to stop tolerating and start doing. You need to do the things you know you should.

It's time to start thinking, "What if I could actually change this part of myself? What if I could actually unfuck myself?"

When you're hit with that decision between getting down to work and continuing to goof off on your phone, instead of thinking "I'm just a procrastinator anyway" and resigning yourself to that path, what if you made a conscious effort to challenge that assumption?

When you're faced with a situation that would normally make you nervous, such as speaking in front of a crowd or going on a first date, what if you didn't allow yourself to back out just because you're having thoughts of "I don't want to do this because I lack confidence."

What if you could just do it instead?

The Greek philosopher Epictetus summed it up nicely: "*First say to yourself what you would be; and then do what you have to do.*"

It's pretty straightforward: if you want to get a better job or make more money, figure out what you need to do, whether it's getting better qualifications, starting your own business, or honing your skills through study and practice.

And then do it. Don't tolerate a life of "I'm not smart enough" or "I don't fit in" even when those very thoughts are running through your head. Remember: you are not your thoughts.

Do what you have to do. Take the steps necessary to be what you would be—and stop tolerating the person you think you are.

TIME TO GET TO WORK

> *There is nothing to writing.*
> *All you do is sit down at*
> *a typewriter and bleed.*
> —*Ernest Hemingway*

This is an opportunity for you to empty some of the conversational contents of your brain onto paper. What lands on the page will include various upsets and fears and all kinds of junk that you've become so accustomed to it just melts into the background of "how it is." That's good. Push through it.

What are you tolerating about yourself? What are the things you pretend aren't really a problem or that you're avoiding about yourself, in denial about or somehow trying to overcome about yourself in life?

This includes something as simple as a lack of confidence all the way to the most complicated feelings about your body shape, your drinking habits, your procrastination, your fear, anger, or emotional hang-ups. Do you resent or regret too much? Do you pretend everything is okay when in fact you feel like you're drowning?

Take the time to write down those items you know you need to work on but have never really thought you could.

Q. Write down at least five ways that you feel as if you're "too much." Some examples: "I'm too lazy," I'm too erratic," "I'm too passive," or "I'm too angry." It can be as many as you want, and again, just write until you feel as if you're complete. Your list could include many items, although be careful to recognize if you're just using different words to say the same thing.

I'm too . . .

_____

_____

_____

_____

_____

_____

_____

_____

Q. Explain why you think you are this way. Tell the truth. If you're currently blaming someone else for how you are, tell it like it is for you.

_____

_____

_____

_____

_____

_____

_____

_____

_____

_____

_____

_____

Q. Next up, write at least five ways that you don't feel as if you're enough; for example, "I'm not smart enough" or "I'm not ambitious enough" or "I'm not confident enough."

As before, your list could include many items, although be careful to recognize if you're just using different words to say the same thing or different versions of your first list.

I'm not . . .

_____ enough

_____ enough

_____ enough

_____ enough

_____ enough

Q. Again, why do you think you are this way?
Tell the truth.

_____

_____

_____

_____

_____

_____

_____

_____

_____

_____

Now take stock of what these lists represent to you.
Take a few minutes to look at them in their entirety,
what they mean to you, what life has been like for you.
See if you can track the impact of relating to yourself
in such a way. When you feel like you have a good
sense of what they say about life up to this point,
move on to the next page.

THE EMOTIONAL CONNECTION

Q. What is the first emotion that comes up when you look at these two lists?

_____

_____

_____

_____

Q. How does this emotion physically manifest in your body? (Do you feel a headache, churning stomach, tightness in your shoulders, etc.)

_____

_____

_____

_____

_____

_____

_____

_____

Let that experience in. Allow yourself to be in the presence of these lists and the emotional and physical weight they dredge up.

When it comes to yourself, the words in these lists represent what you are dealing with. That might leave you depressed or numb or angry or whatever, but the straight of it is, this is everything you have been allowing to fester when it comes to yourself. This is what you are trying to fight against every day of your life. The weight, the burden, the drama, suppression, or frustration. The impact on your joy and aliveness. The numbing of a being.

You might be looking at this section and saying "holy shit" right now because it's so heavy, so laden with emotion and overwhelming it seems like just a little too much. Or maybe you're so numb to it that it's having little or no impact on you at all. You've become so accustomed to the burden you can't even see how it's pulling you down; you just know something's off with you. Either way, that's the point—for you to finally see, in black and white, what you have been tolerating about YOU and to be in the presence of what "baggage" really looks like.

Q. What is it really like for you to be yourself in this life? Be truthful; tell it straight. Remember, no one can see this but you. This isn't a pity party, but it is certainly an opportunity for you to be open with yourself.

_____

_____

_____

_____

_____

_____

_____

_____

_____

_____

_____

_____

_____

And yet you keep living this way, which begs the question,

Q. What are the reasons, excuses, and justifications you've sold yourself that have allowed you to continue living life in the way you do?

_____

_____

_____

_____

_____

_____

_____

_____

_____

_____

_____

_____

I want you to consider the idea that you are far more interested in perpetuating the "why" you are the way you are than changing the way you are. Try on the notion that you live this way to avoid something. Avoid what, though?

The first thing that comes into people's minds is usually that they're avoiding something such as "fear" or "pain" or some other negative experience. It's never that. No, really.

I going to propose something radical.

The hook. You're avoiding putting *you* on the hook for yourself AND your life. Whenever you read or hear me talk about responsibility, this is what I'm talking about! Responsibility isn't about blame or fault or paying your bills or driving at the speed limit or whatever other mundane direction we've pointed it in. Responsibility is about getting yourself on the hook for who you are, for your impact and influence; it's about taking ownership of your own emotional skin bag and dealing with yourself powerfully.

How about holding yourself to account for your own joy or confidence or love or peace of mind?

How about holding yourself to account for your own experience of being alive rather than pointing to your past or your shit job, dead town, circumstances, or your whiny friends?

Q. What do you think you get to avoid?

_____

_____

_____

_____

_____

_____

_____

_____

"But Gary, I'm confused/stuck/sad/ [insert your usual explanation here] and I can't seem to shake it off! I want to be happy, but I can't seem to do it!"

Just so you're aware, that's actually an argument _for_ the life you have. The illusion is that you think by explaining your shit, you'll somehow free yourself from it. You won't. When you're in a constant conversation about why you're stuck, you'll embolden and embellish it. It will become the altar at which you'll sacrifice your entire life experience.

Instead of being overcome with trying to *become* happy or confident or powerful, how about *doing* happy or confident or powerful right now?

Y'know, like getting yourself on the hook for this sort of stuff?

UNFUCK SOMETHING, ANYTHING!

Q. Look back at the five items you listed on p. 31. Which one do you think would give you the biggest bang for your buck? That is, which one of these, if you took it on and triumphed, could you point to and say "I unfucked myself" here AND why?

_____

_____

_____

_____

_____

_____

_____

Q. What difference would this make in your day-to-day life? Be specific. How would this change what you do and don't do?

_____

_____

_____

_____

_____

_____

_____

_____

Q. What would a victory in this area of life allow you to do in other areas of your life? That is, what are the implications of you transforming this item? Give this some real thinking. JOIN THE DOTS!

_____

_____

_____

_____

_____

_____

_____

_____

_____

_____

_____

Q. What is one new action you could consistently take that would be a demonstration of your being victorious with yourself?

_____

_____

_____

_____

_____

_____

_____

_____

Q. In what way would this new action be a triumph over what you have been tolerating about yourself?

_____

_____

_____

_____

_____

_____

_____

_____

_____

_____

_____

_____

_____

_____

PEOPLE, GET READY

Before you start the parade, don't kid yourself. If there's a chance for you to fuck this up, you will. If you've ever tried to lose weight, you'll know exactly what I'm talking about here. The problem is we usually spend so much of our lives undermining, sabotaging, and shrinking from living a big life that when those predictable patterns return we get derailed or disappointed or sometimes even tempted to return to old and predictable ways. How do we interrupt this stuff?

Easy. We first get straight about what's predictable. No la-la bullshit about hope or determination or this-time-it's-different-no-really-it's-different-no-I'm-serious-this-time-really.

Stop kidding yourself.

You have to see the *whole* picture. The life you are aiming for and all of the ways that you'll talk yourself out of it when it gets too hard, too boring, or too inconvenient. Look back at how you've handled this situation in the past, and use that to predict how you would do it again in the future. Only then can you head it off at the pass. We are too reactive; it's time to get proactive.

Q. Look to how you've handled this item in the past. Now, how might you predictably undermine yourself with this item in the future? Why do you think you do this?

_____

_____

_____

_____

_____

_____

_____

_____

_____

_____

_____

_____

_____

Q. What are the typical thoughts you have when undermining yourself? (Be specific.)

_____

_____

_____

_____

_____

_____

_____

_____

_____

_____

_____

_____

_____

_____

_____

_____

Okay, can you see it now? Can you see the ways in which you'll sabotage yourself?

The key to stopping this behavior is this: rather than saying what you'll NOT do when that arises, it's important for you to say what you WILL do (i.e., some new action you will take) to interrupt the drift of your automatic. Wouldn't you rather have a real and powerful say in how this life goes instead of drifting away on autopilot?

Q. Name one new thing you could do when faced with these predictable thoughts and behaviors.

_____

_____

_____

_____

_____

_____

_____

_____

_____

This is where you get to make a promise, but before you do: Remember what I said about promises earlier? You will never get anything important accomplished in your life, you'll never unfuck anything if you do not start to develop a profound relationship to whatever you promise yourself. You need to reinvent what promises mean to you. They need to become personal contracts that include specific terms, conditions, what-ifs, by-whens, and a thick layer of I-don't-think-I-can-do-it to give you some incentive to grow! Let's do that now.

YOUR PROMISE

I hold myself to be accountable for being _____

_____

_____

_____

and promise to _____

_____

_____

_____

as a real-world demonstration of my commitment.

Whenever I feel compelled to return to my past behaviors and patterns I promise to _____

_____

_____

_____

_____

_____

_____

_____ instead.

It's important that you don't rush this work. If you're still trying to figure out what the things are in your life that are fucked up and why that is, spend some time here. Reflect on the questions and exercises we've just walked through. Then write it here.

DEBRIEF

What I learned about myself from this section is:

_____

_____

_____

_____

_____

_____

_____

_____

_____

_____

03

PROJECT 2: THE RELATIONSHIP TRAP

*In this life, you'll sometimes have to do things you don't want to, with people you don't like, and in **places you don't care for.***

—Unf*ck Yourself, p. 87

We all have at least one relationship in our life that doesn't work and no, not the one you have with yourself; we just did that section, remember?

Maybe you don't get along with your dad or your neighbor. Maybe your love life doesn't have the magical spark it used to. Perhaps your boss is a jerk. Or you haven't talked to your sister in months or even years. That insult or lie they told you, or the way they live or talk has been stuck in your thrapple like an old chicken bone for quite some time now, huh?

Some of our more fucked-up relationships can be really bad. Nasty, even. Maybe you're at each other's throats, jockeying to be right and win the war; perhaps it has even come to blows or gone straight into the welcoming and eager arms of your lawyer. Then there's the gossip, angst, fury, and precious emotional room that these take up in your life. Just thinking about that other person can completely fill your body with anger, pain, or frustration. That's *all* completely worthwhile, right?

Maybe you were dumped or ignored or treated in a way you feel wasn't fair or right, and the resentment, sadness, and loss of power are running your life. Just so we're clear, by the way, that's called being a victim. How's that working out for you?

Last, there are those other relationships that are just kind of, well, dead. Maybe it's that neighbor of yours whom you see only once in a while or that family member where there's just no traction, nothing happening, a desert in a once-plentiful and meaningful connection. You drag that weight along with you every day and pretend everything's fine (plenty of coffee helps) when in fact there's no aliveness, no vitality, no real connection. In truth, you're mostly just numb about the whole thing.

Perhaps that thing they did was the last straw for you, but you don't have the guts to close it with some sense of peace or acknowledgment, so you're willfully letting that relationship rot until it just withers and dies like the medieval amputation of a once-gangrenous toe. Ignorance is bliss or time heals all wounds or whatever bullshit you've told yourself to pacify the guilt and avoid the effort of what it actually takes to connect with another or separate with some kind of honor and genuine peace of mind.

And how do we deal with those dead relationships? We tolerate them, of course.

Have you ever really thought how much weight relationships have on your quality of life? Perhaps you have, and you've overhyped how you feel about that relationship to the point of paralysis. Or perhaps you've ignored it to the point of neglect or willful ignorance. Pick your poison.

Often we'll try to "fix" our relationships, but what we're really doing is a hack job at trying to change the other person, to grind them into submission to become more like the person we want or think they *should* be. We think, if only Ashley weren't so cold and self-centered, if only Dad wasn't so judgmental, if only Matt wasn't so irresponsible, if only Laura stopped nagging so much, and on and on and on. If only, huh?

The new insanity is trying to get others to be different so you can be your best self. Good luck with that one.

It never works. Trying to change the other person never works regardless of how much you've convinced yourself it does, not unless you're secretly committed to having others quietly (or otherwise) resent *you* for the rest of your life. Now, THAT works!

And when we're all out of ideas, when we've tried everything we can to fix or change the other person, that's when we resign ourselves—not consciously of course—to just deal with it. We go through our whole lives with one, two, or even half a dozen dead relationships in the background of our thoughts, and we've resigned ourselves to think that's just the way it is.

Many of us look at our relationships like a fast weekend in Vegas. In the end, we hope we win more than we lose. We think we'll eventually come out on top. If you could see how you've actually stacked the odds against yourself, you'd see you're already fucked. Vegas loves you, baby.

Just look at modern dating, for example.

That feeling of meeting someone you really click with, that giddy high of falling in love/lust—or at least something close to it, even if the relationship ultimately ends in failure, helps you forget about all of the previous relationships that crashed and burned from the word "go." Yet, like any weekend gambler, you keep going, carried forward by the few odd wins you have. Eventually it's the hope that kills you.

How the hell did we end up this way? Why on Earth are we so bad at our relationships?

I'll tell you. Because on a fundamental level, we don't know how to be in them.

IT ALL GOES BACK TO THE BEGINNING

The only tips you ever picked up about relationships were from watching everyone around you during your childhood. You could pick any one of your current relationships and find that it's modeled around one of a handful of primary ones from when you were a kid.

How you related to your parents, Grammy and Pappy, your competitive older brother or your nerdy younger sister, your playmates or your first-grade teacher, those primary connections formed the entire bases for the relationships you have today as an adult. Oh yeah, and you have the same primary emotional reactions in these relationships too. Your boss doesn't listen? What is the model? Your mom? Your brother? What's your reaction? An upset five-year-old? A resentful teen?

Your partner doesn't care? Who are they modeled around? Your dad? What's your reaction there? You'll see the same primal complaints and emotional triggers for those early relationships being played out as an adult. It's no wonder the shit doesn't work.

We've all heard the cliché of men being "mama's boys" and women having "daddy issues." It's so fucking boring and lacking in intellectual effort. All of your basic relationships as a kid are affecting your current reality—because this stuff is powerful!

And we're all affected by it. Everyone is modeling their adult friendships and love life and business connections around the methods they learned when they were a kid. It's actually hilarious to watch someone throw a stroppy tantrum at their missing stapler or wet towel or edgy email. Your life is like one giant WTF at times!

There's nothing quite like observing a human being try to tackle the complexities of an adult life with the emotional depth of a bowl of soup. Of course, as a kid you got over your upsets with the remarkable dexterity of an Olympic gymnast. These days you grip onto them like a curmudgeonly old fart, whether you realize it or not.

Maybe it's not as obvious to you in your life as with some people, but it's there. Your adult relationships don't work because you don't know how to have adult relationships. You were never taught (no one was, so stop blaming), and you haven't figured it out in the meantime.

So how do you fix that? How do you unfuck your relationships?

Q. First, make a list of all the relationships in your life that aren't working. Maybe there's one big one that comes to mind, or a few people where your relationship isn't working as well as it could.

_____

_____

_____

_____

_____

_____

_____

_____

_____

_____

_____

_____

_____

_____

Q. Why are these relationships this way?

_____

_____

_____

_____

_____

_____

_____

_____

_____

_____

_____

_____

_____

_____

_____

_____

Next, take stock. How have all of these relationships negatively impacted you as a whole? Let it all in.

Q. When you look at this list, what are the emotions that best describe your experience?

_____

_____

_____

_____

_____

_____

_____

_____

_____

_____

_____

_____

_____

_____

Q. Focus on this emotional state for a moment. Where in your life is this a recurring emotion?

_____

_____

_____

_____

_____

_____

_____

_____

_____

_____

Q. When you are in this emotional state, what do you typically do? What are the actions (or lack of action) most closely associated with this emotion?

_____

_____

_____

_____

_____

_____

_____

_____

_____

_____

Q. How have these behaviors inhibited the
direction of your life and success?

_____

_____

_____

_____

_____

_____

_____

_____

_____

List the "top three," the relationships that you feel are currently the greatest drain on your aliveness and/or peace of mind.

1. _____

2. _____

3. _____

Now, if you could unfuck one of these relationships, which one would give you the biggest bang for your buck? Why? Do NOT use your relationship with yourself in this section.

_____

_____

_____

_____

_____

_____

_____

_____

Great—this is the relationship we're going to unfuck together!

Q. If this relationship was finally unfucked, what could you do or be that you currently feel you're not free to do or be?

_____

_____

_____

_____

_____

_____

_____

_____

_____

_____

The relationship I am out to unfuck is my relationship

with _____.

The following are some of the most important ingredients you will need to unfuck any relationship. Depending on your situation, you might need to adopt some or all of these. Regardless, complete each section fully and with no lies, withholds, or pretenses. Remember, this is an opportunity to confront yourself. That might well include some discomfort or unease at what is getting revealed by the work you are doing. In short, tell the truth to yourself.

ACCEPTANCE

Acceptance is brought to life by you. It's a self-generated grace you grant yourself to illuminate real peace of mind and human connection. It's a state where we can all take a breath and allow someone or something to just be itself without the need to alter it; change it; or hell, sometimes even interact with it. In short, we let that situation or person just *be*. Often, in our most contentious relationships, we are irked by the things that the other person says or has said, the way they act, character traits or behaviors that we think "shouldn't be." In reality, those are all things we just don't *accept* about that person. That's right—you've become the kind of person who is not okay with someone else being themselves!

Judgmental much? Being an accepting human being means you are open to allowing others to be who they are. Judgment, resentment, or whatever else is currently fueling you will eventually be your undoing.

I'm not speaking in a vacuum here. I am well aware of what it takes to finally accept someone. I devoted years of my life to quietly blaming my mum for how things had turned out for me. My punishment (although I didn't know it at the time) was to distance myself from her, to be stingy with my whole self, to reveal myself in very small doses to her. I had become a resentful, angry, and disconnected man. I had spent so much time focusing on what I thought my mum should have done or shouldn't have done that I completely lost sight of what she actually did do.

Until it hit me.

She gave me life. I got my shot at being alive. She did the most important part. The rest is now up to me. I know, I hear you, "Yeah, but what about the way I was raised?"

You can choose to have that shit be as relevant as the eggs you had for breakfast this morning or significant enough to model everything you do from here on out. The choice is yours. Whichever one you choose could well go on to be the making of your life.

Recently I was watching my eldest son play football (soccer, to the barbarians) on an otherwise ordinary Tuesday night. I noticed the whir of my thoughts, the worry and pressing concern for the BS of my life, what I needed to handle, the annoyance for this thing, and the unease about that thing. I just wasn't present.

But I caught myself, and right there, at that moment, I suddenly imagined that my life was about to end. No, really—I got connected to the idea that this was my last night on this Earth. That my final breaths were counting down. Suddenly I was struck by the urge to suck this all in, to pause and take in every nuance, every last detail of my surroundings. Everything slowed. I had a momentary plunge into sadness, and then a profound stillness awoke within me.

I experienced the trees sway and surge in the gentle night air, the joy and passion of my son's voice calling for the ball, spending the vigor of his youth so lavishly and carelessly in the pursuit of victory. I sensed my lungs expand and contract, the comforting, hollow thud of my heart against my ribs, and then I remembered:

I'm alive.

I said it out loud: "Thank you for this, Mum. Thank you for all of this."

After doing some hard work in this area, I can truly say I now accept all the people in my life just the way they are, but none more so than my mum. I accept her, and I love her without condition. She is who she is, and I choose to love all of that, not just the easy bits.

Being an accepting human being means you are open to allowing others to be who they are. I mean, FFS if you can't contort yourself to that bare-bones minimum of common human decency, how in the hell will you ever make your relationships work?

That's right, you won't. So saddle up, Bucky, we've got some work to do!

Q. What have you been unwilling to accept about this person in your life?

_____

_____

_____

_____

_____

_____

_____

_____

_____

Q. What has been the impact on you AND them from taking this position?

_____

_____

_____

_____

_____

_____

_____

_____

_____

_____

Q. What do you need to give up, which point of view or "truth" do you need to release to accept this person just the way they are?

_____

_____

_____

_____

_____

_____

_____

_____

_____

Q. If you are to accept this person, which action would you have to consistently take that would be a demonstration of accepting them just the way they are?

_____

_____

_____

_____

_____

_____

_____

_____

_____

_____

Q. What could you now say to that person that would demonstrate your acceptance of who they are?

_____

_____

_____

_____

_____

_____

_____

_____

Q. Is there anything else you have to give up or release to allow yourself to accept this person?

_____

_____

_____

_____

_____

_____

_____

_____

_____

_____

_____

_____

_____

_____

FORGIVENESS

Your ability to forgive is directly correlated to your peace of mind. Whatever you refuse to forgive lives on in you for as long as you hold onto that thing, and no matter how small or insignificant that thing might seem to you, it gnaws at your joy and satisfaction in ways you can't even begin to see until you finally do forgive.

By the way, save yourself the horseshit drama of "I can't forgive." You absolutely can. You have thus far been _unwilling_ to forgive.

It's that simple. Your capacity for forgiveness is infinite. Your willingness for it is where you get stuck.

However, let's put something to bed about forgiveness once and for all. Forgiveness has nothing to do with letting people off the hook for their BS. It doesn't mean you've been used or duped or taken advantage of either if you do choose to forgive.

Also, forgiving someone doesn't make you better than they are. That's called self-righteousness, my friend.

Forgiveness might require you to see someone's humanity, to look past what they did or didn't do, and rather than seek to compare it with what you would do or would have done, understand where they were coming from given their life, their humanity, and their circumstances. Forgiveness is finding that humanity in those you have failed to forgive and relating to them as something other than your story about them.

As a footnote, forgiveness does not mean you are opening the door for the same sort of behavior as the past from either you or them. It might also include your taking a stand for what you are willing to allow or not allow in your life. It's completely possible to forgive and let go and to do it without any sort of cynicism, resentment, anger, or loss of who you are.

Let's get some forgiveness on.

Q. What have you been unwilling to forgive?

_____

_____

_____

_____

_____

_____

_____

_____

_____

_____

_____

Q. What impact has this unwillingness to forgive
had on you and your life?

_____

_____

_____

_____

_____

_____

_____

_____

_____

_____

_____

At this point you are left with a stark choice. You can continue to hold onto your views and opinions of others, or you can reach for something greater. What might be a bit different this time is the idea that you are absolutely clear what this choice now is—a life of resentment, anger, frustration, and being a victim, or a life of freedom. Choose.

Often, in the aftermath of authentic acceptance and forgiveness, people are left with a question: "What now?" Unfucking any relationship will require you to relate to that person from a new place. Think of this workbook as your opportunity to wipe the slate clean. That will also require you to write something new, something more empowering and enlivening.

Q. If you take on the idea that your existing relationship with this person comes from what you haven't accepted or forgiven (which is in the past), what would take the place of that lack of acceptance or forgiveness now and in the future?

_____

_____

_____

_____

_____

_____

_____

_____

_____

_____

_____

_____

_____

COURAGE

This is the last piece you'll need to unfuck a relationship and, in my opinion, usually the most challenging. You see, making real change in your relationship requires *you* to change. It requires you to be different, to walk into the same familiar environments and "show up" in new ways. This might look like saying things or responding in ways that people aren't used to. You might be kinder, more assertive or expressed, more loving or compassionate, all of which might require you to step outside of how everyone in your life automatically sees you. And that takes courage.

The courage to stand there, in the face of everything, and be judged or ridiculed or criticized. But know this—that's the case with every step of a personal transformation.

When you're out to reinvent yourself and your life, you'll need to do the work to get others on board with your new vision for yourself. Never criticize or demean them for doing what human beings do when faced with a new and uncertain reality—they try to find the familiar and certain. And, like all human beings, they will do that by any means necessary, even if it means cynically undermining something potentially great.

It's your job to forgive and accept them too.

Epictetus once said, "'My brother shouldn't have treated me in this way.' Indeed, he shouldn't, but it's for him to see to that. For my part, however he treats me, I should conduct myself toward him as I ought. For that is my business, and the rest is not my concern. In this no one can hinder me, while everything else is subject to hindrance."

Stop worrying about what the other person is doing and start focusing on how you can learn to be in that relationship.

If a love relationship or a friendship is truly unworkable, if it's in complete breakdown and no longer serving anyone, then get out of it. If it's unfixable, then end it. I know that comes with a plethora of problems and possibly some monumental change, but that's just how it is.

Remember, most people would rather be miserable than deal with what it takes to make themselves happy. Don't be that person! It's a complete sellout on yourself and everyone else when you double down on your own misery. You're probably not the only one in your life who needs a fresh start.

If a family relationship is in the same condition, you need to start to map out what will work. Chopping your family down is never a good idea no matter how extenuating your circumstances might be. Agreeing to disagree is a start. We're not all supposed to see life the same way. That's kinda how it works. You can be straight about what you are willing to allow in your life (without judging or blaming others or losing your shit) while standing for having a family that *works*. You might be the lone voice for this, but it's far better to have a lone voice for what's possible than to sheepishly join the cacophony of discord and complaint arising from a forest of finger pointing and murky black-arts espionage carried out in the silent fury of a text message or muffled telephone conversation. Just because some people agree with a viewpoint does not make that viewpoint "the truth." In reality it's only something you have agreed with another (implicitly or otherwise), and some of those agreements are just plain nasty no matter how justified they might seem.

For fuck's sake, be the one, be authentic, be real, but most of all, be kind. If your "truth" demonizes or diminishes others, you might want to give that a second look. Might I suggest having your truth be about something a little more uplifting for everyone involved, no matter how slighted or damaged or self-justified you might feel.

But if you're arguing a little more than you'd like, don't talk as much as you used to, or can't seem to find time for each other, find the solution. And the solution comes from changing your typical ways of being, from coming from a different place when you interact with this person.

It could be you just need to shut up every once in a while and listen. Or maybe it's the opposite. Maybe you're always holding back, resenting, and turning yourself into a victim, and now you need to open up a little more. It's possible to speak about what's going on with you without being a victim or blaming others. You do know that, right?

Often it really works to actually spend *more* time with the other person, to make the effort to connect, to reach out and get into their world, a passenger seat on their fleeting journey through this life. People aren't nearly as fucked up as we're led to believe. Just because someone doesn't make sense to you doesn't mean they don't make sense to someone else. It's just too easy to start tagging them as a weirdo or that there's something wrong with them and all of it born out of your frustration from being unable to relate.

If you want to fix this, you have to make a change.

The actions I am taking with _____
that demonstrate my acceptance of who they are and
my forgiveness for what they did or did not do are:

_____

_____

_____

_____

_____

_____

_____

_____

What I now need to take ownership of myself and my
reactions in this relationship is:

_____

_____

_____

_____

_____

_____

_____

_____

_____

_____

It's time to step up, expand your relationship game, and make a promise to yourself. If you really want to take ownership of fixing this relationship, write out those specific terms and then hold yourself to that!

YOUR PROMISE

In this relationship I now promise to be:

_____

_____

_____

_____

_____

_____

Whenever I am tempted to react or return to my usual default behavior in the future, I will:

_____

_____

_____

_____

_____

_____

_____

_____ instead.

What was uncovered about your relationships in this section that surprised you? Have you been living for too long thinking that you could just never see eye to eye with that person, and now you realize, maybe that's not true? We can't do life alone. This shit is important. Perhaps it's time for you to get invested in the idea that only you can make a relationship go the way you want it to and that that begins and ends with you *being* who you need to *be*. Maybe you could even dampen your ego and make that phone call you've been avoiding.

DEBRIEF

What I learned about myself from this section is:

_____

_____

_____

_____

_____

_____

_____

_____

_____

_____

_____

_____

04

PROJECT 3: PURPOSE, WHAT PURPOSE?

The most successful among us got to where they are today **because they transcended obstacles.**

—Unf*ck Yourself, p. 147

It seems the bullshit bombs are everywhere on social media these days when it comes to the subject of purpose.

We're constantly being sold an idea, a tonic for all our woes, a promise to help you "find your purpose." It's fast becoming the modern-day snake oil, and the business is, apparently, very good indeed.

Buy this course, follow this account, sign up for this newsletter, do this workshop, or join this community and all for $29 a month or a onetime fee of $499 to learn the tips and secrets that will help you in your worldwide pursuit of the one thing that all the smart people have but apparently you don't. It seems your purpose is out there just waiting for you. Somewhere.

Fly your purpose-seeking ass to the beaches of Thailand or become a world-renowned professional surfer or write for your favorite high-end magazines or meditate with animals on Instagram. I mean FFS, where does it all end?

Purpose, purpose, purpose. We're fed a hearty diet of how much we need it, how our lives will only ever be complete and fulfilled once we find it. If only *you* had purpose, you'd love every last minute of your life, brimming with gratitude and aliveness and every day would be nothing but sunshine and rainbows and cool unicorns, right? Find your purpose and you'll never work a day in your life. Ugh.

There's a major flaw here. This apparent "search" for purpose (it must be a search since you're supposed to find it) leaves you with something a little less empowering than it seems at first glance.

Think about it. If you're searching for your lost keys or your missing phone or that elusive sign on the highway (and don't get me started on "looking for love"), it's not like you're lit up like a Christmas tree, filled with possibility and life-inducing purpose juice, is it? No, you're usually agitated or annoyed or worried or some other negative experience of yourself. Why? Because you are looking for something you don't currently have but that you are certain you need *and* if you don't get that thing, something bad is going to happen. No wonder everyone is so worked up about this purpose shit!

Finding your purpose has become an *external* answer to what is fundamentally an *internal* question. You're unhappy, you're unfulfilled, I get it. But what makes you think the answer to that is *out there*? I know, I know, according to this cool person on social media (who looks like their shit is together), they "found" their purpose making jewelry from old shoes and cocktail shrimp tails and not only are they all calm and shit, but they're loaded now too!

This search for purpose has led you on a wild goose chase, like you're some kind of Indiana Jones character climbing through remote jungles and ancient, booby-trapped temples for that mystical holy grail: YOUR purpose. Like there is only one for you, and dammit, you better find that sucker!

And once you lay your weary eyes on it, you're going to become immediately enlightened. As you step out of the shadows on that glorious day to slowly remove your purpose from its holy golden plinth, your hands trembling with excitement, the angels will sing, you'll be filled with the ecstasy of the ages, and your bank account will receive an instant transfer from the universe because you are at one with it all and everybody else can go fuck themselves.

Suddenly your life is now about frolicking with orphaned baby koala bears in the outback and using your downtime to finger-pick your one-of-a-kind acoustic guitar (handmade by Peruvian artisans in a small workshop snuggled in the ruins of the Machu Picchu), to a YouTube audience of millions, while all the other idiots will be stuck in their cubicles at the call center wishing they had done that damn course with you.

Because, of course, your "purpose" is always portrayed as something radically different from what you're currently doing, often as something completely outside the box. I mean, you can't live your purpose in *your* neighborhood or in that sucky job of yours, right?

Not if you go along with the purpose monkeys, that's for sure.

Had enough yet? Look, it's all just BS, and while I'm sure somebody somewhere came up with the idea of "purpose" to inspire people, it has mostly become yet another syrupy gimmick in an already complex and testing world.

So what exactly are you supposed to do? If meditating in the deserts of Arizona or diving among the corals of the Great Barrier Reef isn't the divine answer to living a life of purpose, what is?

Well, let's take a look, shall we?

It's probably best to define purpose before we get too deep into this. I'll go with the dictionary definition:

> **pur·pose:** *the reason for which something is done or created or for which something exists.*

Hmmm . . . the reason for which something (namely you) exists. Or, more accurately, a compelling and inspiring reason for you to truly live rather than just exist or survive. Something that empowers you to powerfully live—purposefully. An irresistible context for being alive.

Or as I like to say, for you to live *on purpose*. What would it look like for you to actually live with purpose? Who would you be? What would you be doing?

To start, you're going to list all the areas of your life in which you feel you lack direction or fulfillment or aliveness, or the areas where you feel a general sense of going nowhere. Pay special attention to those areas where it feels like you are wasting your time or spinning your wheels. Be specific here: do not generalize, but instead itemize your life. Bear in mind that this list can include anything, including career, body, finances, or love life, but it has to come from the life you *have* and not the one you *want to have*.

Q. Where specifically in your life do you feel there is something lacking?

_____

_____

_____

_____

_____

_____

_____

Q. In terms of having the most negative effect on you, list the three areas of life that you feel do not reflect how you want your life to go and, in each case, clearly state why you think these areas are the way they are.

_____

_____

_____

_____

_____

_____

_____

_____

_____

Q. When you look at these three areas of life, what is it like for you to experience them as they currently are? Be specific. What is it like for you to get up in the morning and face a life like this? What is the weight or impact on your day-to-day life, and how are you limited by your life being this way?

_____

_____

_____

_____

_____

_____

_____

_____

_____

Q. What do you sacrifice about yourself by having life be this way? What is this costing you?

_____

_____

_____

_____

_____

_____

_____

_____

_____

Q. If your life keeps going in this direction, if you take away the illusion of hope or optimism, how do you predict your life will turn out in two, three, or five years?

_____

_____

_____

_____

_____

_____

_____

_____

_____

_____

_____

_____

It's pretty obvious that this is something that has to change, right?!

Look over the areas that you listed where you feel something is lacking. Now pick the one area you are choosing to bring to life.

I am committing to bring purpose to _____

_____

_____

_____

_____.

INTENTIONAL INTENT

You see, the point here is to start taking on specific areas of your life with some kind of overriding intent. A commitment to turn off the autopilot you're currently coasting on. To be alive to your potential, eager to make a difference. To no longer just go along with the bullshit. To step out there and take a stand for what really matters to you. A point to everything that you do.

To live with purpose.

Let me give you one of my favorite and most inspiring examples of someone who lives with purpose.

My wife.

When my eldest son was about seven or eight years old, I was traveling a lot for work, and my wife did all the running around with him. And I mean ALL of it. Even if you set aside the litany of stuff she handled at home, from bills to laundry to cleaning and everything else, there was still football, tae kwon do, school, birthday parties, homework, practice, doctors, dentists, you name it, she was shuttling that kid around for miles and miles, seven days a week, week after week, month after month, from this event to that event, scrambling for the right clothes, snacks, dealing with the traffic, teachers, instructors, teammates, weather, you get the picture, right? Oh yeah, and we had a newborn then too.

I was constantly amazed at the ease and grace with which she got it all done. I mean, people all over the world are doing this kind of stuff but it's grinding them down, they're burned out and resigned and teetering on the edge day after day. I needed to know her secret, for the love of God!

So I asked her.

And she told me.

"Here," she said as she nonchalantly handed me her phone with the calendar app open.

I excitedly scanned the screen and the list of appointment after appointment, all organized, and immediately I just assumed that's the answer. She's organized.

"No, you goofball, lots of people are organized. Open one of those appointments," she said.

So I did. And there it was staring me right in the face. Her reason for being alive. Her purpose.

It said, "Football practice—5:30 p.m. to 6:30 p.m." (nothing extraordinary about that, right?), but then just below in capital letters it proudly proclaimed, "CREATING A MAN."

Shit. That's what this is about? She's really creating a man! Our son.

It hit me like an errant train. The lump in my throat grew; I was moved by the commitment and clarity of purpose she had created for herself. My eyes welled up with the surging emotion. This is it? This is what all of this is about? All the hassle, all the driving, coaxing, and coaching, making sure the calendar is up to date and the snot is wiped and the drying of tears, one-woman-taking-on-all-the-BS suburban warrior, this is what is fueling her?

It turns out she's just like everyone else. She gets deflated, she gets overwhelmed and stressed and slips onto autopilot just like you do. And then she reminds herself of her purpose, what this life of hers is about, right there in a moment of running ten minutes late for school or scrambling for quarters at the toll booth.

She's *creating* a man. That's what ALL of this is about for her, every single moment of her life is a full-on commitment to *her* reason for being alive. The one she put together and laid as a foundation for all she does. It's what gets her out of her bed and into her life. I should add that she created this purpose *after* our son was born as something to invigorate herself and raise her game. It most certainly wasn't a divine spiritual gift bestowed on her from some nebulous source of the universe or something. She quite literally made the fucking thing up.

And all these years later, she's still living that purpose. It inspires her, she gets lit up by the challenge and settled by the reminder that this is what it's all about. All day. Every day. This woman loves her life and what she's up to in it, and she created the whole damn thing herself.

Just like you can.

FROM FANTASY TO PURPOSE

Look at that area of life you picked earlier, and you'll see the gaping hole. There's no purpose, no real point to it. There's an absence of inspiration, of aliveness, and of the kind of magnetism that draws a person out of the autopilot we all too easily get sucked onto.

Why? Because you never created any. Most people believe that inspiration comes *at* you, not *from* you and that, my friend, is a superstition. Inspiration is created and expressed; it's not to be hunted down or found somewhere under a rock in the Himalayas.

"But Gary, the Himalayas *are* magical and mystical and amazing. I'd LOVE to go there! You don't know what you're talking about!"

Oh, be quiet, Captain Stardust.

Right now, there's someone eking out a meager existence in the dry and stingy air of those magical, mystical mountains who is completely unfulfilled with their life and dreaming of the day when they can move to the United States to drive an Uber in the opulence of downtown Baltimore or the leafy quiet of an oxygen-bloated Wisconsin suburb.

In short, inspiration and purpose are both self-generated.

Me? The purpose of absolutely everything I do is *to make a difference for people.*

I do it at the grocery store, with my kids, my neighbors. If I'm talking to you, I'm working out how I might make some kind of difference in your day. A kind word; a helping hand; hell, sometimes it's just eye contact and a smile. It's what I've devoted my entire life to, and I love being this guy.

It's the reason why I write books too, by the way.

So, what about you (and let's keep this simple)? What could you make your life about in the area you picked earlier? (Hint—the more you make it about yourself, the more challenged you'll be by the circumstances. The more it's about impacting what's going on around you, the more empowered you'll get.)

Q. What is something you could make this area of your life be about?

_____

_____

_____

_____

_____

_____

_____

_____

_____

_____

_____

_____

_____

_____

Q. If you made this your purpose, what would you do differently (like, really DO differently, with new actions, new responses, etc.)? Keep in mind, this is about what you will do now rather than what you won't do anymore.

_____

_____

_____

_____

_____

_____

_____

_____

_____

Q. If you allowed this purpose to spread to other areas of your life, what areas would be most significantly affected and why?

_____

_____

_____

_____

_____

_____

_____

_____

_____

Q. By being true to this purpose, what kind
of human being would you get to be that you
currently do not experience yourself as?

_____

_____

_____

_____

_____

_____

_____

_____

Q. What are the roadblocks (typical behaviors of yours that are self-destructive/indulgent or otherwise negative) that might get in the way of this purpose and that you'll now have to be vigilant about?

_____

_____

_____

_____

_____

_____

_____

_____

Q. When the compulsion to act in this way arises, what will you do instead that is more aligned with your purpose?

_____

_____

_____

_____

_____

_____

_____

_____

_____

Q. How will you know you have been successful in
realizing your purpose every day?

_____

_____

_____

_____

_____

_____

_____

_____

_____

_____

YOUR PROMISE

Understanding that this newly stated purpose shapes everything I do, I promise . . .

_____

_____

_____

_____

_____

_____

_____

_____

_____

Whenever I am tempted to react or return to my usual default behavior in the future, I commit to

_____

_____

_____

_____

_____

_____

_____

_____

_____

_____ instead.

In the words of the Roman philosopher Seneca, "The greatest blessings of mankind are within us and within our reach. A wise man is content with his lot, whatever it may be, without wishing for what he has not."

Now, that doesn't mean you shouldn't seek to improve your life. It doesn't mean that you can't make radical change by reinventing your career or moving to another country or throwing yourself into some new passion or other. It simply means that the rut you find yourself in has less to do with your circumstances than it does with how you view and handle it.

Purpose—what your life is about—is always at stake.

With that in mind, perhaps it's time to start giving some thought to what your life would look like if you lived it more purposefully.

Q. Let's start with your career or business. If you were to start living with some clear intention, a spine from which you find inspiration and clarity, would you work the same hours or more or less? Would you put the same amount of effort and focus into your projects, or does having a purpose shift your attention?

_____

_____

_____

_____

_____

_____

_____

_____

_____

_____

_____

_____

Q. Start thinking about how your day would change if you were living with purpose. How you'd spend your free time, how much pride you'd take in your work, how you'd interact with your boss or clients or co-workers. How could you bring some life to these seemingly "ordinary" aspects of your life?

_____

_____

_____

_____

_____

_____

_____

_____

_____

_____

_____

_____

_____

_____

Q. This applies to your social life as well. How would your dating or intimate relationships change if you approached them with some real intention? Would you spend more or less time with your parents or children or friends?

_____

_____

_____

_____

_____

_____

Q. Again, run through your normal routine in your mind, and imagine what it'd look like if you made that change. Your hobbies apply here too. How do you spend your free time? With a more purposeful life, how would that change? Maybe you'd spend more time with your hobbies. Or waste less time on stuff that doesn't contribute to living your life with intention.

_____

_____

_____

_____

_____

_____

_____

_____

_____

_____

_____

_____

_____

A PURPOSE GREATER THAN YOURSELF

It's all internal. You already have the ability to live life on purpose. You just have to change your thinking a bit.

When the purpose you create is greater than your day-to-day petty concerns, you are called to be. Be what? Be bolder, be more influential, be more outgoing or decisive or loving or industrious. When you have a purpose for what you are doing, it raises the bar of your participation in life. You are compelled to reach, to stretch, and to go beyond your most base concerns.

> *This is the true joy in life, the being used for a purpose recognized by yourself as a mighty one; the being a force of nature instead of a feverish, selfish little clod of ailments and grievances complaining that the world will not devote itself to making you happy.*
> —*George Bernard Shaw*

In many ways, this single quote says it all.

Your purpose comes from you—it's an invention, a dare you present yourself with and that you'll have to remind yourself of over and over as you occasionally slip into the ordinary stream of mindless conversations and behaviors that most of us do when going about our lives. You have to hold yourself to account for your own purpose; no one is coming to save you or lift you up or inspire you. That's your fucking job.

What I learned about myself from this section is:

_____

_____

_____

_____

_____

_____

_____

_____

_____

_____

05

SEVEN ASSIGNMENTS

I believe you can change your life. I also believe it's a lot of hard fucking work. Here's what's important: the more you understand what you are up against, the more power you'll have to recognize and transcend that shit.

I want to prepare you for reality, for the weight of disappointment and the predictability of your self-sabotage and for you to be aware and ready to deal with yourself in the most critical moments.

Maybe you're lost or confused or looking around your circumstances and you feel that this is fucking hopeless. Whether you drink too much, drug too much, sex too much, lie too much, spend too much, or hurt too much. Whatever your thing is, I want you to know you can change your life and you can change it right now. At this very moment.

And so I want to leave you with seven life-changing assignments. You can take them on in whichever order you wish. Each assignment corresponds to a chapter in *Unf*ck Yourself*, so I'll lay them out in the order of the chapters. I thoroughly recommend reading the specific chapter before embarking on the corresponding assignment.

Each assignment is based on the assertion that I encourage you to take on. If you remember from *Unf*ck Yourself*, assertive language is the kind of language that cuts through the bullshit and demands something of you.

I also recommend working through each of these assignments for at least a full day, but you could even take as long as a week, or a month, or more. Go at a pace that works for you but certainly not one that's immediately comfortable. The ferocity with which you embrace these assignments will determine how powerfully you can create real and lasting change in your life. That ferocity *has* to come from you. If you bring that kind of energy and commitment, the assignments will open up a world of change. Fail to do so and . . . well, you know the story by now.

1: "I AM WILLING"

You realize you have the life you're willing to put up with, right? So let's put this into practice.

Look at your calendar right now. Pick a day when you will bring either a sense of willingness where there has been none or take a stand for what you are no longer willing to put up with. The entire day, every moment that you are awake, do it. No backing down. Handle your entire life (relationships, health, finances, career, organizing, unfinished business of any kind, basically whatever comes to mind) from this standpoint of willingness during that period.

There is something important for you to discover here. Ultimately everything in your life will come down to this assertion of being alive for you or not.

DEBRIEF

What I learned about myself from this assignment is:

_____

_____

_____

_____

_____

_____

_____

2: "I AM WIRED TO WIN"

Consider everything in your life as a win. Even when you're losing, it's a win for some subconscious programming. What could you accomplish if you focused that hard wiring for victory onto something of your own choosing?

Choose an area of life where you feel as if you have been losing. Dig into it and uncover the answer to this question: "What have I *actually* been winning here?"

See if you can observe what point gets proven by having your life be the way it currently is. Who do you blame or hold to account, AND what do you avoid about the state or direction of your life?

When you clearly see what you have been winning, which area of life are you now going to bring this hard-wired winner to bear on?

DEBRIEF

What I learned about myself from this assignment is:

_____

_____

_____

_____

_____

_____

_____

_____

3. "I GOT THIS"

We often fool ourselves into thinking life is too much or that somehow we're just not equipped to handle the tougher challenges. Yet if you look back on your life you'll see a litany of testing circumstances that you triumphed over. No matter how tough it gets, you got this both then and now and long into the future.

Take on one thing in your life that you have been actively avoiding or resisting. Past taxes? Old credit card charges? Cleaning your closet or garage? How about that email in-box or stuff you need to sell? Charge into it and deal with it. Do not pause, do not hesitate: handle it. Be a demonstration to yourself of how powerfully you can deal with the clutter of life.

DEBRIEF

What I learned about myself from this assignment is:

_____

_____

_____

_____

_____

_____

_____

4. "I EMBRACE THE UNCERTAINTY"

Human beings are addicted to certainty. The problem is, it doesn't exist—it's a myth handed down from generation to generation. To succeed in this life will require you to embrace this world of uncertainty and fight for the life you really want.

This one assignment could change the entire trajectory of your life. This is about bringing to life a long-buried dream or passion or aspiration. That thing that has niggled at the back of your mind and comes up from time to time only for you to suppress and suffocate it until it dies down again.

Name that dream. Dig into it, begin to put together a strategy for making this dream become a reality. No more what-ifs, no more buts or one-days, this is it. This is your time. Awaken yourself. I can't save you; no one can but you. You're either going to do this thing of yours or you're not, and here's *my* coaching: step out into the great unknown; fucking *do it*.

DEBRIEF

What I learned about myself from this assignment is:

_____

_____

_____

_____

_____

_____

5. "I AM NOT MY THOUGHTS; I AM WHAT I DO"

Most people give too much significance to what's going on in their heads. They follow a trajectory of self-doubt; fear; considerations; and plain, old-fashioned superstition. Life only changes in the paradigm of action. That's it. If you want to change, do differently than you did before. You are not your thoughts. ACT!

You can have a lot of fun with this one. Spend a single day doing whatever you typically would not. Eat in *that* restaurant, buy *those* pants, say *that* thing, hug someone, call an old friend, book that ticket, apply for that job . . . you know the score. By the end of the day you should have completed at least four tasks that you would NEVER usually do. Step out of the everyday noise of your head and ACT!

DEBRIEF

What I learned about myself from this assignment is:

_____

_____

_____

_____

_____

_____

_____

_____

6. "I AM RELENTLESS"

Relentlessness is a force of nature that is available to all human beings. It's easy to take your life on when you're enthusiastic or excited or determined. But what do we do when all that's gone? Be relentless.

This is an awareness assignment. Start to get keyed into the various elements of your everyday life that have flatlined. Engage with the idea that you mostly operate in life well within the hallowed "comfort zone."

What would it look like for you to start doing what you do at higher level? Take some time to jot down your thoughts about this. Think what it would look like for you to constantly operate outside your comfort zone, and write down what that would look like.

DEBRIEF

What I learned about myself from this assignment is:

_____

_____

_____

_____

_____

_____

_____

7. "I EXPECT NOTHING AND ACCEPT EVERYTHING"

Our lives become muddied and confused by the constant pressures of expectations. The problem is, we can't really see that the worst expectations are the kinds we ourselves put into the mix. Real freedom and power emerge when you free yourself from the self-imposed prison of expectations.

This assignment is to be done over a seven-day period. Put a reminder in your phone twice per day with this assertion, once at noon and once at 6:00 p.m. When you see the reminder pop up, deal with what you are doing from the perspective of this assertion. Say to yourself, "I expect nothing and accept everything."

This is an opportunity to bring some real peace of mind into your life. If you're worried, anxious, pissed off, or generally just not okay with how things are, this assertion will highlight where you are not accepting or are just hung up on your own expectations. You have to accept where your life is to have any real say in changing it.

DEBRIEF

What I learned about myself from this assignment is:

_____

_____

_____

_____

_____

_____

_____

06

CONCLUSION:
A SEE-YOU-SOON
KIND OF FAREWELL

This is your life. Right here, right now, and you have a choice. You can either indulge your shit and repeat it until you die or finally take yourself on in a way that actually changes your life. There's no in-between. It's one or the other. Take responsibility for your experience of being alive. If you're fucking miserable, own it. Step up the ownership of where you are and where you are headed. Can't come up with a pathway?

Create one.

Right now.

Look at where you are most unhappy and declare a change. Get to work. Too overwhelming? Get to work. Too hard? Get to work. Too complicated? Get to work. Do something, do *anything*, even in small increments. Change happens when you begin to change what you do. Everything great that has ever happened in this world began with a small action. It was followed by another and then another and then another. For the most part, that's just how we get things done as human beings.

The only thing that's "stuck" about you is what you talk about. Period. You and everything about you persist in a landscape of conversation that you've become so addicted to, you can't see the woods for the trees.

You are not who you think you are. You're not a set thing, locked into the tissue of your organs or trapped in the minutiae of your plasma. You are not your toes or your hair or your eyes. You are most certainly not your past. You are not your middle school or your dad or that neighbor who fucked with your head.

You are not your personality or your worst habits or your stutter or your "generous" arse. You are not your embarrassments or your shame or your guilt or your anger or even your beliefs. You are none of these things.

You *have* thoughts, but you are not your thoughts. You *have* a body, but you are not your body. You *have* a past, but you are not your past, and it's a criminal waste of a life to whittle the wondrous marvel of what it is to be alive down to a few primary complaints and shitty habits only to one day turn to face the mounting pile of uninspired years and weeks and months and days with the cold realization that you have so very few of those left to make this life of yours a truly memorable one.

You are a space for life to happen, a wild and wondrous environment for miracles and hardships and everything in between. You are a moment, a loud bang in a burst of time that trails to a whisper and then disappears into the abyss.

As I like to say, you are a fucking miracle of being, and it's finally time for you to start acting like one. Do the work.

See you on the flip side.

About the Author

Born and raised in Glasgow, Scotland, Gary moved to the United States in 1997. This opened up his pathway to the world of personal development, specifically to his love of ontology and phenomenology. This approach, in which he rigorously trained for a number of years, saw him rise to become a senior program director with one of the world's leading personal development companies. After years of facilitating programs for thousands of people all over the world and later studying and being influenced by the philosophies of Martin Heidegger, Hans-Georg Gadamer, and Edmund Husserl, Gary is producing his own brand of "urban philosophy." His lifelong commitment to shifting people's ability to exert real change in their lives drives him each and every day. He has a no-frills, no-bullshit approach that has brought him an ever-increasing following, drawn to the simplicity and real-world use of his work.

To fully DO THE WORK and accomplish the change your life requires, start here: